FLORISTS' REVIEW
wedding
BOUQUETS

DESIGNS BY TALMAGE MCLAURIN, AIFD

FOREWORD

Today's weddings are more than just ceremony. They are
fabulous parties and personal expressions of taste. As soon
as the date is set, excited anticipation leads to countless
hours of planning to make the event a unique expression
of the couple's love and happiness.

Both fragile and elusive, freshly cut flowers enhance this day
like nothing else. An understated nosegay of fragrant *Freesias*,
a dramatic cascade of exotic orchids, a timeless cluster of
garden roses, each personalize the wedding day with exquisite
gifts from nature—lending graceful notes to memories and
images that will last a lifetime.

Filled with inspiration for both the bride
and the florist, *Wedding Bouquets* is
Florists' Review's fifth book devoted
exclusively to wedding flowers. It is
arranged by color and includes easy-
to-understand how-to information
throughout. It is also filled with stylish
ways to create a perfect flower-filled day.
And that begins with what most girls
have dreamed about from childhood
– their wedding bouquet.

TALMAGE MCLAURIN, AIFD

TABLE OF CONTENTS

blush PINK fuchsia

Romantic and feminine, *pink*

has personality that can go from

sweet to sassy and a style

that will suit any of the four seasons.

Long tendrils of trailing vines, clipped from a potted ivy plant, cascade from this ravishing profusion of fragrant Oriental lilies. Composed simply and elegantly, this classic bouquet has timeless appeal. A floral-foam-filled bouquet holder ensures the blooms remain hydrated and vibrant.

PREVIOUS PAGE:
Both light and dark colors intermingle in this loose, gardenlike composition of 'Majolika' spray roses, *Hydrangeas*, *Hypericum*, *Freesias*, *Veronica* and *Trachelium*. Long streamers of double-faced satin ribbon, in lavender and green, add the finishing touch.

Wrap waterproof tape around the handle of a soaked bouquet holder, adhesive side out.

Adhere pieces of heather to the tape, and bind with beading wire.

how-to ▶

Arrange spikes of heather into the bouquet holder in a radiating manner to form a collar.

OPPOSITE PAGE:
Inside what appears to be an entirely organic composition, the mechanics for this grand botanical nosegay – a straight-handled bouquet holder – are beautifully concealed. The "posy holder" is composed with spikes of heather that are wrapped with beading wire. A spiky heather collar accessorizes the grouping of roses and red-tipped huckleberry.

A glistening snowflake ornament makes an elegant
armature for 'Lea Romantica' spray garden roses.
The pearly snowflake tips add a dramatic wintry collar,
and the frosty effect is echoed in the dusty miller
accents. Metallic mesh tube ribbon shimmers softly
beneath the diminutive creation.

Clip several spray rose
blossoms, and wire and
tape them to elongate
their stems. Insert the
wire stems through the
snowflake ornament.
Tape the stems together
with stem wrap.

Insert three heavy-gauge
hairpin-shaped wires
through the group of
wire stems, just above
the tape binding, to make
a stronger handle. Bind all
wire stems with stem wrap.

how-to ▶

Wire lengths of mesh tube
ribbon onto the handle,
and tape with stem wrap.

Though comprising only two rose varieties – 'Yves Piaget' and 'Helga Piaget' – this compact hand-tied bouquet projects a grand appearance. The bare stems are wrapped in a luxurious coordinating satin ribbon, for a tailored finish.

Roll long pieces of aluminum wire into spirals using needle-nose pliers.

Bend the ends of the wires down, so the spirals are somewhat horizontal, and gather them into a "posy."

how-to ▶

Arrange the fresh florals through and around the wiry accents. Take care to conceal the wire "stems."

OPPOSITE PAGE:
A lovely hand-gathered bouquet of miniature callas, sweet peas, Guernsey lilies (*Nerines*) and globe amaranths (*Gomphrenas*) gains hypnotic appeal with multiple swirls of pink aluminum wire. The wires appear at first to be arranged among the blooms but actually are assembled beforehand, as an armature.

Although uncommon bridal flowers, exotic pink *Anthuriums* are stunning in this contemporary bouquet, which is particularly suited to tropical and seaside ceremonies. Alongside the *Anthuriums* are pink carnations, yellow *Freesias* and *Solidago*, surrounded by loops of lily grass wrapped with gold bullion wire. The ends of the grass blades are attached to wired wood picks and inserted into the floral foam.

Spray adhesive on the leaves, then press them onto a disc (a flange from a bolt of ribbon or a disc cut from foam-centered board or cardboard).

how-to ▶

OPPOSITE PAGE:
This high-fashion bouquet features pale-pink 'Juliette Droues' French garden roses, which beautifully contrast the vibrant geranium leaves that cover the circular collar. Clusters of dark feathers accent the flowers and foliages, and a garland of *Camellia* leaves that are stitched and wired together offers additional motion through the center of the composition.

'Lea Romantica' spray garden roses star in this coordinating boutonniere, corsage and pomander set. The exquisite blooms are accessorized by sprays of beads and beaded blossoms, the crimson hues of which unite the peachy roses with the ruddy *Gerbera* centers featured in the pomander. Assembled as an elongated corsage, the little lady's personal flowers create an exquisitely tailored detail on her gown.

Bend a chenille stem into a large "V" shape, and insert a small wood pick into the crook. Twist the chenille stem to bind the pick.

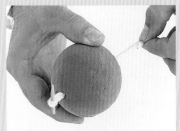

Insert the ends of the chenille stem into a saturated floral foam orb, and pull the chenille stem through the orb. Form a loop with the two ends of the chenille stem through which the ribbon handle can be threaded.

how-to

Wrap the twisted portion of the chenille stem with stem wrap so water is not wicked from the foam sphere. Tie a braided ribbon handle through the loop, and arrange the floral materials.

OPPOSITE PAGE:
A riot of blooms converge in this colorful and textural bouquet, which maintains a romantic and demure appearance with its limited use of foliage. Spray roses, tulips, orchids, *Lisianthuses*, hyacinths, *Veronicas* and *Ranunculi* are arranged in the decorative bouquet holder.

This luscious tapestry of blooms and hues results in a modern, sophisticated bouquet highlighting a professional florist's artistry. Roses are blended with pastel-hued *Gerberas* and fragrant *Freesias*, and the composition is encircled by a feathery collar of plume *Celosia*. A satin-covered bouquet holder completes the splendid bouquet.

Starting at the bottoms, wrap *Gerbera* stems with ribbon. Secure the first rotations with glue, if desired. Knot the ribbon just beneath each bloom, and leave a long streamer.

Tie a second length of ribbon just beneath each bloom, to create a total of three streamers on each. Assemble the *Gerbera* into a bouquet, and bind the stem bundle with clear tape.

how-to ▶

Cover the clear tape with a wrapping of ribbon, and secure it into place with several pearl-headed corsage pins, which also add a decorative "jeweled" enhancement.

OPPOSITE PAGE:
Cheery *Gerberas*, embellished with delicately sheer organza ribbon streamers and stem wrapping, offer a romantic accompaniment. Because *Gerbera* blossoms are likely to droop without proper hydration, start the ribbon wrapping about an inch above the ends of the stems, so the flowers can be stored in shallow water without damaging the ribbon. Just before the ceremony, neatly clip the unwrapped stems.

This "designer" bouquet is carefully crafted to maintain a precise monochromatic color harmony. Bicolor 'Sarwell' spray roses and two varieties of miniature callas are surrounded by deep burgundy *Coleus* accents, which take the place of green foliage. **Tip:** *Coleus* is prone to wilting, so hydrate it overnight and allow it to "harden" before use. When arranging, carefully hand-tie the delicate leaves along with the other materials because, even after hardening, the stems may remain fragile. Store and deliver this bouquet in a water-filled container.

Wire each *Camellia* leaf using the stitch-wiring, or sewing, technique, and tape with stem wrap. Tape some leaves together in pairs.

how-to ▶

OPPOSITE PAGE:
A delightful hand-tied bouquet of garden and spray roses brims with texture and fragrance. *Camellia* leaves provide natural-looking accompaniments to the roses but offer a sturdier option than the roses' more delicate foliage.

A few ribbon roses are tucked among the fresh 'Mariatheresa' garden roses in this striking bouquet, which also incorporates *Ranunculi*, parrot tulips, *Veronicas* and heather. The permanent blooms provide an "upsell" opportunity. Offer to custom-create some for the bridal attire or bridesmaids' bouquets or as keepsakes for the wedding party.

Cut a length of wire-edged ribbon. Grasp both ends of one edge's wire and pull, gathering that edge of the ribbon into the center of the wire.

With the gathered edge at the base, begin rolling the ribbon to form the rose. Continue until the flower shape is complete.

how-to

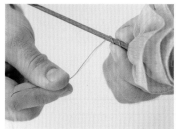

Place the "rose" atop a wood pick, and twist the ribbon's wires around the pick to secure.

OPPOSITE PAGE:
Delicate blush-hued spray roses, with their beautifully open blossoms, make a grand statement and are accompanied by deep pink *Hypericum* berries and extra-long, wide taffeta ribbon streamers in this hand-tied bouquet.

Rather than risk damaging customers' purses, create your own faux pocketbooks to fashionably hold blossoms. Here, inexpensive craft foam forms a *Galax*-leaf-covered pouch that holds a wealth of Guernsey lilies (*Nerines*), which are in water tubes hot-glued inside the bag. **Tip:** To avoid pollen stains, remove the anthers from all pollen-bearing blossoms, such as the Guernsey lilies.

Fold a sheet of craft foam in half, and cut the foam into the desired purse shape.

Staple the sides to form a pocket. Remove the stems from *Galax* leaves, spray the backsides with adhesive and layer them onto the pocket.

how-to ▲

Punch holes into the corners of the open end of the pouch. Thread two lengths of quarter-inch ribbon through the holes, and tie to form "straps."

OPPOSITE PAGE:

An exquisite collection of *Cymbidium* orchids, more lavish than could be utilized in a corsage, makes a chic wedding floral accessory. The blooms are placed into water tubes, which are hot-glued to the bag's interior. The glue likely will damage the bag's interior, so stock an assortment of attractive yet affordable purses from which customers can choose.

blue PURPLE lavender

A traditional wedding accompaniment,
blue and its royal cousin,
purple, transform any bouquet

into a singular statement.

Covered with a fringe of crystals and sliver-shaped sequins, this evening bag becomes a lovely holder for blue *Hydrangeas* and miniature *Phalaenoposis* orchids. The flowers are discreetly tucked into water picks, which are positioned in plastic foam that is glued into the bottom of the purse.

PREVIOUS PAGE:
Combining varied hues into a striking palette that transitions from powder blue to purple ensures that this bouquet will complement bridesmaids' gowns of any indigo shade. Creamy *Ranunculi* nestled into the nosegay's center add depth and dimension while softening the tone-on-tone drama of the grape hyacinths (*Muscari*), sea holly (*Eryngium*), *Agapanthuses* and *Veronicas*.

Cluster individual branchlets of baby's breath into a bouquet, and trim the blooms to create a uniformly mounded shape. Glue all other floral materials into the mound of baby's breath with floral adhesive.

how-to ▶

OPPOSITE PAGE:
Featuring a mound of baby's breath as its foundation, this charming tussie-mussie offers an affordable way to include orchid blossoms, in this case *Dendrobiums*. The premium florets, along with *Delphinium* blooms, *Hypericum* and geranium buds, are individually glued to the mass of baby's breath.

Tulip *Anthuriums*, arranged so their backsides form a striking collar, give incredible dimension to an elegant nosegay of 'Ocean Song' roses, waxflowers and keepsake flower-shaped jewel pins.

Saturate the foam of a large bouquet holder. Apply floral adhesive to the stem of a tulip *Anthurium*, and insert the stem into the bouquet holder, so the spadix points downward. Continue around the holder to form a collar.

Bend aluminum wire to form a long series of loops. Fold the wire loops into a square, and place them into the base of a small box, if needed, as a "mold" in which the wire can be shaped. Insert two lengths of wire into the bouquet holder, and secure to the wire frame.

how-to ▶

OPPOSITE PAGE:
When premium flowers are desired but cost-prohibitive, suggest brides use a few standout blooms, such as these *Phalaenopsis* orchids, supplemented by attractive foliage and an eye-catching collar – in this case lamb's ears (*Stachys*) foliage and a striking wire frame that provides visual rather than physical support.

This lavish garden gathering, in near-complementary lavender and apple green hues, is a pretty pick for spring and summer. 'Mari Romantica' spray garden roses, 'Cool Water' roses, parrot tulips, hyacinths, *Viburnums* and lilacs offer fragrant abundance, with jewel-encrusted rose accents adding a bit of sparkle.

Wire individual salal leaves using the stitch-wiring, or sewing, technique. Tape the wire stems with green stem wrap.

Design the hand-tied bouquet, making sure all the stems are parallel. Arrange the wired-and-taped salal leaves into the underside of the bouquet. Bind the stems with waterproof tape.

how-to ▶

Wrap the bundle of stems with organza ribbon, top to bottom to top, as many times as required to create a smooth surface. Push pearl-headed corsage pins, at an upward angle, into the ribbon-wrapped stem bundle as accents.

OPPOSITE PAGE:

The stems in this round, mounded nosegay of *Freesias* and lilacs are wrapped in matching lilac-hued ribbon adorned with pearl-headed pins, creating a luxurious space for the bride to grasp the bouquet. Green *Hypericum* berries, which are buried among the blooms, provide contrast in color, form and texture.

A lush nosegay of massed miniature callas showcases a natural grouping of related hues. *Aspidistra* leaves, rolled to mimic the shapes of the callas, create a collar that neatly finishes the bouquet in an inventive yet cost-effective manner.

Cut each *Aspidistra* leaf in half horizontally, then roll each leaf piece into a calla shape. Attach steel picks to the rolled leaf ends, and arrange them into the floral-foam-filled bouquet holder.

how-to ▲

OPPOSITE PAGE:
Ravishing jewel-toned *Delphiniums* and stocks, in an analogous harmony of crimson and purple hues, are accessorized by a boalike fringe of deep blue peacock feathers. A delicate silver-hued bouquet holder completes the decadent composition.

Aluminum wire in a coordinating magenta hue creates a continuous coil around a rich assortment of jewel-toned 'Moonlite' carnations, Gerrondo *Gerberas*, 'Amalia' roses, bachelor's-buttons and coral bells (*Heuchera*) foliage. The flowers, which are arranged into a crystal-like bouquet holder, are grouped by type for impact.

Trace the outline of a large vase or other circular object onto foam-centered board. Then trace around a smaller circular object in the center of the larger circle. Cut out the discs with a craft knife, discarding the smaller circle.

Hot-glue one end of a piece of ribbon onto the foam-centered board disc. Wrap the ribbon through the center of the disc in random fashion, covering it completely. Hot-glue the end of the ribbon to the disc to secure it.

how-to ▶

Place the bouquet holder into the middle of the ribbon-covered disc. Dip the end of the bouquet holder's handle into hot-melt (pan) glue, and secure it into a decorative holder.

OPPOSITE PAGE:

The ribbon-wrapped bouquet collar, sumptuous ostrich feather accent and lavish nosegay call to mind an elegant, classic chapeau. The 'Old Dutch' roses, Gerrondo *Gerberas*, miniature carnations and drumstick *Alliums* are arranged in groups for maximum impact, and coral bells (*Heuchera*) foliage lends additional texture.

Blades of lily grass – the first items to be inserted into the bouquet holder – form the outline of this updated cascade. Their fringy character is an unexpected backdrop for the gorgeous blossoms of 'Cool Water' roses, 'Moonshade' carnations and *Aranda* orchids.

Dip the handle of a bouquet holder into hot-melt (pan) glue, and secure it into a decorative holder.

Dip permanent *Magnolia* leaves into hot-melt (pan) glue, and affix them to the underside of the foam-filled bouquet holder, to conceal the plastic base.

how-to ▶

Arrange carnations in a lavish mound formation, starting in the center of the bouquet holder and working outward.

OPPOSITE PAGE:
Striking bicolor carnations go from basic to upscale when used in unexpected ways. This radiant mound, encircled by permanent *Magnolia* leaves and secured inside a textural posy holder, reveals the fascinating character of these enchanting flowers.

chartreuse GREEN forest

Nature's neutral, *green* has
an organic and contemporary
aesthetic that succeeds as the star
of these verdant bouquets.

Dramatic groupings of florals and decorative elements highlight each segment in this nouveau nosegay of 'Limbo' roses, *Dendrobium* orchids, 'Green Trick' *Dianthuses* and lily grass. Shiny aluminum wire creates the artistic elements, and a wire-wrapped handle continues the lustrous lime theme.

PREVIOUS PAGE:

Naturally elegant *Echeverias*, green-and-peach carnations, wispy 'Green Trick' *Dianthuses* and premature *Hydrangeas* incorporate both warm and cool green hues in this earthy collection surrounded by *Galax* leaves. The *Echeverias*, which are placed carefully to avoid overpowering the bouquet with their visual weight, can even be reclaimed from the bouquet and propagated for a lasting, living keepsake.

Bend a length of aluminum wire to resemble a pair of leaves on a long stem. Use needle-nose pliers to create a pointed tip on each wire "leaf."

Coil one end of the wire around a pencil to form a spiral into which the *Cymbidium's* stem will be inserted.

how-to ▶

Adhere one end of the shaped wire to a wood pick with stem wrap. Insert the wood pick into the bouquet holder, and arrange the orchid blossoms.

OPPOSITE PAGE:

Grand *Cymbidium* orchids, accented by *Camellia* foliage and *Hypericum* berries, are assembled into a modern cascade bouquet using decorative aluminum wire. The tumbling effect could have been achieved with a traditional wire-and-tape method, but the jaunty tendrils add a playful and unexpected twist.

Classic ingredients of *Hydrangeas*, *Hypericum* berries and preserved maidenhair fern combine here for an ethereal accompaniment that has a delicate appearance but sturdy construction. Button-backed pearl-headed pins mirror the dainty *Hypericum* berries while adding a distinctive sheen to the collection.

Dab floral adhesive onto each button, and insert a pearl-headed pin through the buttonhole. Apply floral adhesive to the tips of the pins, and insert them into the floral foam.

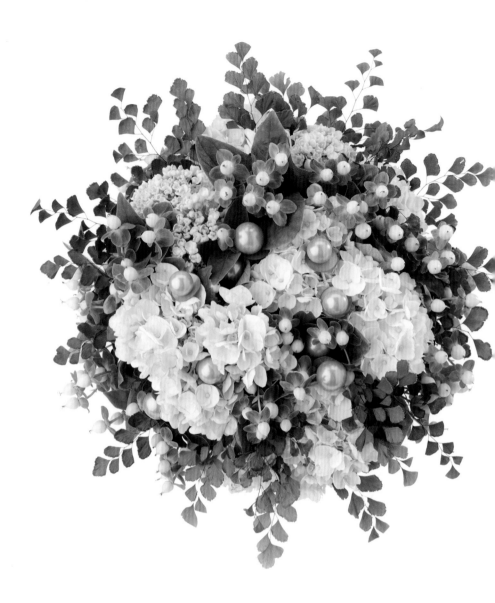

Insert sprays of *Dendrobium* orchids into a saturated bouquet holder. Bind the sprays with bullion wire to form an inverted "cone." Shape the small end of the *Dendrobium* cone to add a bit of curve.

how-to ◗

OPPOSITE PAGE:
An exquisite mass of sparkling bejeweled 'Navona' Asiatic lilies is elongated by a lush inverted "cone" of *Dendrobium* orchids, many still in bud stage. The exotic cascade is bundled with bullion wire and shaped into a dynamic curve.

Adding foliage to the base of a bouquet holder is the simplest way to create a bouquet collar. Here, *Ruscus* leaves surround an all-green grouping including 'Super Green' roses, carnations, bells-of-Ireland, *Echeveria* and *Hypericum*. A single blade of lily grass, wrapped with silver bullion wire, encircles the bouquet, and heart-shaped jewels add sparkle.

Gather three callas, and bind their stems with waterproof tape to form the central "bloom." Clip several furled calla spathes from their stems. Unroll the spathes, and tape each one around the perimeter of the central bloom in multiple layers. Conceal the tape with ribbon. Roll calla tips under.

how-to ▶

OPPOSITE PAGE:
Formed of massive 'Green Goddess' callas, this tiered composite creates the illusion of a grand single bloom or a royal scepter. A jeweled pin affixed at the beribboned binding contributes to the regal air.

Four miniature *Cymbidium* orchid blossoms compose this grand pocket square. Cut a thin piece of cardboard to fit the pocket, and apply the blooms with either spray or floral adhesive, making sure no adhesive will come in contact with the fabric.

A clutch purse is accessorized with a trio of pretty *Hydrangea* florets that are simply sprayed with adhesive and applied to the handbag. With this fast and elegant technique, the purse remains functional, but the treatment is best employed on inexpensive bags because adhesive residue may remain after the blossoms are removed.

Cut individual leaves from a permanent poinsettia blossom.

Attach each poinsettia leaf to a wood pick with stem wrap. Then arrange them into the bouquet holder.

how-to ▶

Dip additional leaves into hot-melt (pan) glue, and adhere them to the underside of the bouquet holder to cover it.

OPPOSITE PAGE:
Glittering permanent poinsettia leaves offset this captivating mix of *Cymbidium* orchids, roses, carnations, *Hydrangeas* and *Hypericum* berries. Sprays of ivy extend the drama. Permanent poinsettia leaves are available in a range of hues, offering myriad ways to personalize this concept.

peach ORANGE rust

Flavorful hues, from *peach* to *orange*, capture a range of moods, adding just the right touch of sugar or spice to a bouquet.

All the way from the Florentine Renaissance era comes the well-known della-Robbia style, interpreted here by the mixing of kumquats and spray roses in an attractive nosegay. The eye-catching combination is enhanced with the verdant geranium leaves and *Hypericum* berry accents. **Tip:** Add fruits at the last minute, if possible, because the ethylene gas they emit reduces the lifespan of many flowers.

PREVIOUS PAGE:

Hand-tied in a tightly compacted mass, this glorious bouquet calls to mind an elegant, richly hued tapestry. The rare finds of sun-drenched ocher callas and golden kangaroo paws (*Anigozanthos*) join lemony yarrow and ruby *Hypericum* berries.

Bore a hole through a foam sphere with a small wood dowel.

Attach a wood pick to one end of a chenille stem. Insert the chenille through the foam. The perpendicular pick will anchor the chenille at the sphere's base.

how-to ▶

Attach a ribbon handle to the chenille stem at the top, and arrange flowers into the sphere.

OPPOSITE PAGE:

The traditional pomander is "upsized" from its diminutive form, often reserved for flower girls, to a size that is stunning and suitable for brides or their attendants. Soft orange 'Mambo' spray roses and sienna-hued 'Terracotta' roses, along with fresh green *Hypericum* and permanent orange berries, surround the orb.

Grand bicolor 'Estelle' roses, in a terra-cotta hue, are featured along with groupings of diminutive *Hypericum* berries, permanent crab apples and fluffy harvest grasses. Further textural intrigue is added with a soft collar of feather clusters.

Wrap a strip of floral adhesive around the base of a foam-filled bouquet holder. Secure the holder inside a decorative bouquet cozy.

Arrange roses and permanent materials into the foam-filled bouquet holder. Gather grasses into groups of three or four, and attach steel picks to them. Arrange the grasses among the florals.

how-to ▶

Tuck feather sprays around the base of the bouquet to form a soft, dimensional collar.

A furled swath of vibrant orange mesh encases this delightful cluster of roses, tulips, miniature *Gerberas* and lamb's ears (*Stachys*) foliage with a shimmering aura. The ribbon's sassy dovetails are curled to replicate the tulips' flared petals.

Saturate the foam in a bouquet holder. Gather a mass of mesh fabric around the holder, and secure it to the holder's handle with waterproof tape. Shape and swirl the fabric around the holder's foam, and pin the mesh to the foam with hairpin-shaped wires.

how-to ▲

OPPOSITE PAGE:
Realistic feather butterflies and moth orchids (*Phalaenopsis*) flutter through this distinctive cascade bouquet. The spray of orchid blossoms, left intact, spills from within a cluster of citrus-hued roses and *Ranunculi*, and hanging *Amaranthus* accentuates the waterfall effect.

Enhancing a resplendent hand-tied bouquet of fresh roses and permanent berries, a russet-hued velvet poinsettia plant is disassembled and repurposed as a leaf collar. Because hand-tied compositions can be dropped into vases for continued hydration, this design can be made several days in advance and will remain vibrant throughout the nuptial events.

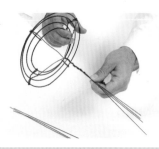

Secure four heavy-gauge wires to a wire wreath, in evenly spaced placements. Twist the wires together to form a handle in the center.

Disassemble a permanent poinsettia, and glue the leaves on the top and undersides of the wire form, in an overlapping manner.

how-to ▶

Hand-tie a bouquet of roses and permanent berries into the center of the wreath, covering the wire handle.

Three varieties of *Mokara* orchids unite in a simple but stunning bouquet based with feathery tree fern. To create depth and dimension, the orchids are glued into the tree fern in stem sections bearing about three florets each. A loose, nearly invisible wrapping of bullion wire adds texture and shimmer.

Arrange two bunches of tree fern into a nosegay formation, and bind the stems with waterproof tape just below the foliage. Trim the foliage to a uniformly mounded shape.

how-to ▲

OPPOSITE PAGE:
Tulips, by their nature, tend to resist precise, formal arrangements, so it's often best to follow their lead. Here they are gathered casually in a striking composition of bicolor blooms, one of which is a parrot variety. A wide striped ribbon, secured with gold-tipped corsage pins, repeats the vibrant palette.

Gathered into a chic mound, this lavish collection of *Mokara* orchids, 'Surprise' sweetheart roses, carnations and *Hypericum* berries gives a modern twist to a traditional style. A sleek and sophisticated bouquet holder, wire collar and ribbon trim enhance the romance.

Trace the outline of a large vase or other circular object onto foam-centered board. Then trace around a smaller circular object in the center of the larger circle. Cut out the large disc and smaller inner circle with a craft knife.

Spray the front sides of sweet-gum leaves with spray adhesive, and adhere them, in overlapping fashion, to both sides of the disc, with their backsides facing up. Spray the disc with copper paint.

how-to

Place the bouquet holder into the middle of the disc. Dip the end of the bouquet holder's handle into hot-melt (pan) glue, and secure it into a decorative holder.

OPPOSITE PAGE:
Fresh leaves clipped from a sweet-gum tree become a textural bouquet collar surrounding a distinctive collection of 'Juliet' garden roses, *Echeverias*, *Sedum* and coral bells (*Heuchera*) leaves. The leaves are adhered to the disc with their undersides facing up to highlight the patterns of the veins beneath the coating of copper spray paint.

Simple and chic, a single-rose boutonniere will hold up under the pressure of many loving embraces. Wide striped ribbon wraps the stem and is pinned in place, with the excess folded over to form a tiny collar.

Assemble grasses into a sheaf, and tailor with a collar of rose blossoms. Insert feathers into the sheaf.

Arrange clusters of *Hypericum* berries between the rose blossoms. Bind the hand-tied gathering with a tight wrapping of waterproof tape.

how-to ▶

Cover the waterproof tape and finish the bouquet by wrapping the stems at the binding point with brown ribbon. Secure the ribbon in place with a corsage pin.

OPPOSITE PAGE:
Ringed by a delicate, monochromatic collar of peach 'Prima Donna' roses and coral-hued *Hypericum*, this feathery sheaf of plumelike grasses and pheasant feathers is fashionably attired for fall. The arm bouquet, with its organic elements, is particularly suited to informal and outdoor ceremonies.

More than just a purse, this dainty fabric bag is designed as a receptacle for fresh flowers. A plastic-lined, recessed space holds floral foam, which can be hot-glued into place so that the bag still may be opened to access necessities. Here, several stems of peach spray roses top the fabulous accessory.

Adhere lamb's ears (*Stachys*) foliage around a plastic-foam wreath form, in overlapping fashion, with spray adhesive.

Push two heavy-gauge enameled wires, perpendicular to each other, through the foam in the bouquet holder.

how-to ▶

Dip the end of each wire "spoke" into hot-melt (pan) glue, and secure the wires into the inside edge of the foam wreath.

OPPOSITE PAGE:
Soft, velvety accents of lamb's ears foliage provide a sensuous base for a muted pastel palette of *Gerberas*, dried tallow berries (*Sapium*) and *Echeverias*. A dusty-hued ribbon, wrapped around the wreath form and discreetly pinned underneath, creates two cascading tails.

A gorgeous golden garland of wheat grass encircles a harvest of diverse blossoms, from large-bloomed 'Caramel Antike' garden roses, 'Yellow Babe' and 'Mambo' spray roses, and *Cymbidium* orchids to delicate yarrow and gold-centered *Bupleurum*.

Thread *Hypericum* berries onto six individual pieces of thin-gauge wire. Curve four of the wires to form the "loops" of the bow, and leave two of them straight for the bow's "tails," reflexing them to mimic a ribbon's drape.

how-to ▶

OPPOSITE PAGE:
Hypericum berries threaded onto thin-gauge wires make an unexpected botanical "bow" for this playful bouquet of 'Marlene' and 'Mambo' spray roses, miniature callas, *Hypericum*, millet and geranium leaves. The ends of each of the four "loops" and two "tails" are attached to wood picks and inserted separately into the bouquet holder.

An edging of bow-tied ribbon garland, tucked among the roses, daffodils and *Hypericum* berries, lends a sweet charm to this nuptial nosegay. The mellow peach tones are spiced with the daffodils' perky touches of yellow, expanding the bouquet's color-coordinating potential.

Form two small loops at one end of a long strand of ribbon.

Lay one loop atop the other, and pinch, between finger and thumb, where the loops intersect. Fold the top loop under, and tuck it into the opening beneath the pinched area. Tie the loops together.

how-to ▲

Grasp the two loops, and pull the bow tight. On the same strand of ribbon, a few inches from this bow, repeat to form another bow. Continue this process to create the garland.

OPPOSITE PAGE:
Three varieties of spray roses – 'Lea Romantica,' 'Baby Romantica' and 'Gisele Folies' – are presented at varying levels to create depth in this round hand-tied bouquet. This gives the bouquet a casual style that is less rigid than a perfectly round composition, yet it maintains a professional look.

citron YELLOW amber

The color of the summer sun,

yellow is the ultimate

expression of the joyful ebullience

that a wedding day elicits.

This redolent daffodil grouping features a cluster of *Ranunculi* at its center, lending a soft buttercream flavor to the glowing palette. Gauzy ribbon encircles the hand-tied stems, and the trailing ribbon tails keep the look playful and cheery. **Tip:** For sturdiness and maximum eye appeal, insert a chenille stem into each daffodil's hollow stem; the flowers will still take up water, and the stems will maintain their cylindrical shape.

PREVIOUS PAGE:
Stately sunflowers need no additional accompaniment to create a powerful and fashionable presence, as in this simple hand-tied bouquet. Gathered en masse, the field-fresh blooms are at home anywhere from the simplest ceremonies to upscale nuptials.

Tightly roll individual *Galax* leaves into tiny cones. Secure the shape with thin-gauge wire. Insert the wire horizontally, piercing the base of the cone, and bend the wire downward, but don't twist the ends.

Attach a small wired wood pick to the base of each *Galax* leaf cone. Arrange the conical leaves randomly into the bouquet holder as foliage accents to the flowers.

how-to ▶

To add rigidity to daffodil stems, making them easier to arrange into floral foam, cut the stems to the desired lengths, and insert equal-length chenille stems into the hollow daffodil stems.

OPPOSITE PAGE:
This profusion of bright-white tulips and *Freesias* along with sunny yellow daffodils has an opulent appearance and a casual aesthetic. The bouquet's pristine quality is intensified by the limited use of foliage; only a scattering of conical, rolled *Galax* leaves punctuates the mass of blossoms.

Suspended from the primary cluster as a floral tassel, a quartet of miniature callas elongates this radiant cascade composition. A few stems of *Ruscus* provide a verdant transition between the sunny groupings.

Melt a hole in the bottom of a plastic saucer with the tip of a hot-glue gun.

Hot-glue moss to the inside of the saucer, leaving the hole in the center open. Trim the moss even with the edge of the container.

how-to ►

Adhere a dollop of hot-melt (pan) glue around the hole in the center of the saucer, and insert a bouquet holder.

OPPOSITE PAGE:
A collection of nature's bounty is gathered into a moss-covered saucer, which serves as an innovative platform for this monochromatic bouquet. Miniature callas and 'Yellow Island' roses share the spotlight with *Echinacea*, yarrow and a delicate nest featuring a pair of tiny golden eggs.

Sparkling jeweled pins give this multihued bouquet of roses, miniature callas and salal leaves a captivating quality and do double duty in providing extra security to the blooms. Inserted straight into the centers of the flowers, either singly or in trios, the pins extend into the bouquet holder's floral foam.

Make several multiloop bows using ribbon in a coordinating hue. Tie the bows with wire, and twist the wires together. Continue adding bows to begin forming a ribbon sphere.

Tie one bow that will create a loop handle and long streamers at the base. Add this bow to complete the sphere.

how-to ▶

Glue roses and other elements into the ribbon sphere with floral adhesive. Continue adding materials until the pomander is complete.

OPPOSITE PAGE:
Textural sea holly (*Eryngium*) joins a quartet of garden rose varieties to form a colorful, pixielike pomander and matching headband. A plastic headband forms the base for the easy-to-wear hair adornment, to which the blooms are affixed with floral adhesive, and the pomander is light and ready to carry thanks to its ribbon base.

A bounty of textures is emphasized through the dimensional flower placements in this luminous hand-tied bouquet. Fragrant stocks and golden yarrow join a gathering of sunny yellow miniature callas in a glorious grouping.

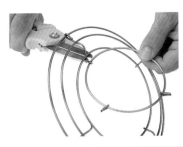

Spray-paint a wire wreath form gold. Clip the center ring from the wreath form using wire cutters.

how-to ▶

Wrap beaded garland around the wreath. Thread additional beads onto bullion wire to create a second garland, and wrap it around the wreath as well.

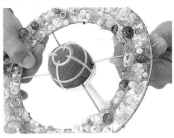

Push a length of aluminum wire through the foam in the bouquet holder, and bend the ends of the wire over the wreath form to attach the form to the holder. Repeat with two additional lengths of wire, creating six "spokes" in all.

OPPOSITE PAGE:
The drama and glamour in this architectural bouquet of 'Sun City' spray roses, *Bouvardia* and *Sedum* is evident from the dazzling beaded collar to the attitude of the roses, as they appear to explode from the base. A wrap of yellow ribbon gives the handle a cohesive look.

Fringed with a handmade feather garland, perky playfulness is added to this grand collection of diminutive *Mokara* orchids and 'Beach' and 'Frisco' sweetheart roses.

Twist bullion wire around the end of a feather. Advance two or three inches along the length of the wire, and twist another feather. Continue this process until the desired garland length is completed. Wrap the garland around the edge of the nosegay.

how-to ▲

OPPOSITE PAGE:
A radiant, citrus-scented 'Toulouse Lautrec' garden rose stars in this sweet accessory for the smallest attendant or flower girl. The wire princess basket is compressed into a narrow, two-dimensional form for more compact carrying, and its handle is replaced by braided ribbon that matches the lush aqua bow.

The stem of an exquisite open 'Citronella' rose is wrapped from bottom to top with plaid ribbon and finished with a ribbon flourish for a charming, modern twist on a classic boutonniere.

Clip *Gerbera* stems short, and don't discard the stem ends. Arrange the blooms into a straight-handled bouquet holder, and bundle the retained stems.

Bind the stem bundle at the top with waterproof tape. Wrap the handle of the bouquet holder with waterproof tape, adhesive side out, and insert the holder into the stem bundle.

how-to ▶

Insert one black-headed corsage pin into the center of each *Gerbera* bloom.

OPPOSITE PAGE:
This gorgeous sphere of *Gerberas* appears to be a hand-tied bundle but actually incorporates a floral-foam-filled bouquet holder to ensure the thirsty blooms show no signs of wilting. Glossy black-tipped corsage pins highlight the flowers' centers for added contrast.

Tiny blossoms of luminous yellow *Mokara* orchids peek out to elegantly accessorize a tuxedo jacket in this floral pocket square. Cut a thin piece of cardboard to fit the pocket, and apply the blooms with either spray or floral adhesive, making sure no adhesive will come in contact with the fabric.

A yarn-covered cardboard disc becomes a modern, textural medallion that is soft with a hint of sparkle. Four tulips, a single carnation and a few *Ruscus* leaves are all that are needed to complete this nosegay. Reflex the petals of the centerpiece tulip for an eye-catching twist on the well-known bloom.

Cover a cardboard disc or a repurposed ribbon flange with a yarn wrap. Apply hot glue to the base of a straight-handled bouquet holder, and secure the bouquet holder into the center of the ribbon-covered disc.

how-to

OPPOSITE PAGE:
A simple hand-tied gathering of citrusy-hued French tulips, bound with basic waterproof ribbon, can be dressed for any occasion. Select the appropriate binding adornment to go from casual to formal. Here, the golden ribbon is secured with a column of corsage pins to suggest a tailored row of pearly buttons.

ivory WHITE cream

The most pristine of palettes, *ivory*
to *cream*, is elegantly bridal

in its simplicity and yet diverse

enough for all tastes.

Hints of color skip through this dramatic white cascade, which uses a trailing *Phalaenopsis* orchid stem as the base through which the 'Jeanne Moreau' roses, parrot tulips, *Veronicas*, lilacs, *Lisianthuses* and *Ranunculi* are woven. Two bejeweled buckles, resembling brooches, add sparkle and keepsake potential.

PREVIOUS PAGE:
Few medleys of blossoms are as elegant or fragrant as this immaculate all-white aggregation. Encircled by hyacinths and *Anemones*, dainty lilies-of-the-valley are clustered in the center for maximum impact. A satin-covered bouquet holder provides a sumptuous handle.

Arrange flowers into a straight-handled bouquet holder. Secure the blossoms with floral adhesive, if desired.

Disassemble two satin bouquet cozies, positioning the two collars onto the bouquet holder. Insert the holder into a complete bouquet cozy.

how-to ▶

Insert three or four shimmery pearl-headed corsage pins into the center of each carnation.

OPPOSITE PAGE:
Ivory-hued carnations and luminous white *Lisianthuses* pair, tone on tone, in a straight-handled bouquet holder accessorized by a three-layer satin collar of deconstructed bouquet cozies. Shimmering groups of pearly corsage pins add sparkle and mirror the beaded cozy handle.

The cascade evolves to a more modern and free-flowing form with a base of ivy upon which peachy 'Cumbia' roses, snowy stocks and satiny golden permanent blooms are nestled. The ready-made ribbon rosettes simply clip into the vining foliage.

Fold a piece of mesh fabric in half, and gather it lengthwise to create a ruffled effect.

Arrange the gathered mesh fabric around the stems of the bouquet, beneath the heads of the flowers, and secure with waterproof tape.

how-to ▶

Loosely wrap additional mesh fabric around the stems of the bouquet, from top to bottom, and secure in place with corsage pins.

OPPOSITE PAGE:
Subtle variations in tone and depth draw attention to this creamy cluster of 'Sandy Femma' roses. The blooms, chosen in several stages of development, are placed at different heights to add interest. Gold mesh fabric encases the stems, maintaining the elegant, monochromatic simplicity.

Romance and whimsy combine in this trend-setting posy of *Phalaenopsis* orchids, which are nestled in water picks among a collection of dried flower pods and curly stems. Yellowed pages from an old book create eye-catching "leaves," which also could be personalized with Bible verses, poetry or the couple's vows.

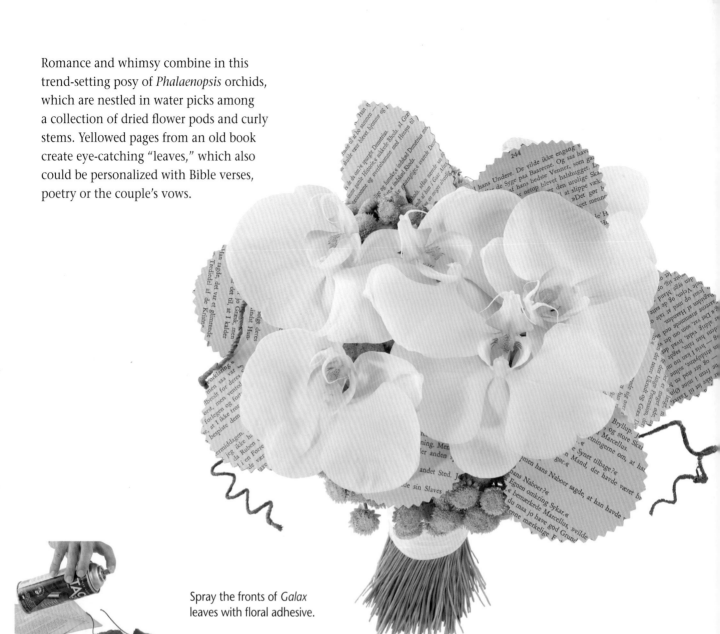

Spray the fronts of *Galax* leaves with floral adhesive.

Press the leaves onto a yellowed page from an old book or a page of the couple's choosing.

how-to ▲

Cut around the leaves with pinking shears to create a scalloped edge.

OPPOSITE PAGE:
Natural and man-made elements surround a gorgeous bunch of 'Cream Prophyta' roses, creating a wealth of contrasting textures. Fluffy permanent *Clematis* pods, pine cones and permanent berries are punctuated by glinting silver-beaded leaves, while a suedelike bouquet cozy adds softness.

CLOCKWISE FROM LEFT:
A trio of *Scabiosa* buds and a single white bloom, from which the petals have been removed, evoke a playful, garden-fresh aesthetic at the lapel. The collection is tied with paper-covered binding wire.

A trio of overlapping silver tree (*Leucadendron*) leaves is simply folded over and tacked in place with a jeweled starfish pin for a tailored boutonniere treatment.

Just a few stems of diminutive lilies-of-the-valley, simply bundled and banded with silver bullion wire, make a stunning accent.

OPPOSITE PAGE:
An abundance of soft green hues punctuates this subtly fragranced, bright-white bouquet. The hand-tied *Freesias*, lilacs and *Veronicas* are surrounded by a ruffly collar of seeded *Eucalyptus*, adding a natural, garden-gathered feel. Pearl-studded ribbon encircles the binding point for a tailored finish.

rose RED crimson

A bold bridal hue, *red* seeks the

spotlight but is able to share

the stage, with incarnations ranging

from demure to daring.

A resplendent hand-tied bundle of 'Freedom' roses bursts from a shower of lily grass in this dazzling bouquet. Painted wooden beads threaded onto the grass blades add the illusion of seasonal berries, making this bouquet particularly appropriate for Christmastime nuptials.

PREVIOUS PAGE:
This breathtaking bouquet features stunning 'Black Baccara' roses and deep crimson *Leucadendrons* complemented by sage-hued *Scabiosa* pods. A burst of dark feather plumes encircling the florid mound conceals the bouquet holder's base and provides a smooth transition from collar to nosegay.

Surround a gathering of roses with lily grass. Bind with waterproof tape.

Wrap one blade of lily grass around the tape to hide the tape, and tuck in or secure the end with a dab of floral adhesive.

how-to ▶

Slide wooden beads onto the blades of lily grass in random fashion.

Peeking from a jacket pocket in ruffled layers, red-tinged *Hydrangea* florets achieve an eye-catching dimensional quality. To make the floral pocket square, cut a thin piece of cardboard to fit the pocket, and apply the blooms with either spray or floral adhesive. Make sure no adhesive will come in contact with the fabric.

Wrap satin ribbon in random fashion around a ribbon flange or cardboard disc sized to the scale of the bouquet.

Fasten the end of the ribbon with a corsage pin.

how-to ▶

Apply hot glue around the center of the ribbon-covered disc, and insert a foam-filled bouquet holder.

OPPOSITE PAGE:
This sassy stylized bouquet incorporates a range of hues from red to burgundy between the *Ranunculi*, carnations, miniature callas and ribbon-encased collar. A colorful conglomeration such as this coordinates perfectly when bridal hues are difficult to match exactly.

Fragrant scarlet 'Francois Rabelais' spray roses mingle with spray chrysanthemums, *Hypericum* berries and *Gerbera* centers, which are accessorized with red-tipped corsage pins inserted through fanciful wire coils, in this petite bouquet ringed with salal leaves. Rose petals affixed to a plastic headband grace the flower girl's neckline.

Select a wire wreath form of desired diameter, and apply a coat of gold spray paint.

Attach 2-inch to 4-inch pieces of holly to the wreath form with bullion wire, completely covering the form. Spray the leaves gold.

how-to ▶

Push a heavy-gauge enameled wire through the foam in the bouquet holder, and bend the ends over the wreath form to attach the form to the holder. Repeat with two additional lengths of wire, creating six "spokes" in all. Spray the leaves gold once more.

OPPOSITE PAGE:
A glitzy gold collar of holly leaves provides a regal accent for a bouquet featuring 'Magnum' roses and preserved *Hydrangeas*. Textural fresh 'Moon Valley' *Pilea* leaves contrast the crimson hues, and a glittery butterfly pick adds another whimsical touch of nature.

Miniature callas are sized right for junior bridesmaids or wee flower girls. Here, they are hand tied and encircled by a sunny collar of goldenrod (*Solidago*). Hairpin-shaped wires create elongated, artificial "stems" for the salal leaves, and the collection of fresh stems and wires is bound with waterproof tape. Ribbon covers the binding.

Pierce a thin-gauge wire through the leaf's rib.

Bend both ends of the wire down, parallel to the leaf, in a hairpin shape. Beginning below the leaf, wrap one end of the wire around the other.

how-to ▲

Starting at the base of the leaf, tape the wires with stem wrap to create a long "stem."

OPPOSITE PAGE:
Sparkling premade wire coils in silver and fuchsia, with co[...] pins pierced through their centers, are grouped together to[...] punctuate this lavish nosegay of bicolor carnations. Used [...] masse, the basic blossoms achieve a dramatic winter chic, [...] used singly they make striking boutonnieres for the gentle[...]

A stunning array of lush 'Chippendale' and 'Piano' garden roses, *Bouvardias* and *Dahlias*, enwrapped with a natural edging of jasmine, brings together a wealth of blushing hues.

Hot-glue a water-soaked straight-handled bouquet holder into a cone-shaped tussie-mussie holder.

Attach a tassel to a wood pick, and secure the pick into the bottom of the tussie-mussie holder with hot glue.

how-to ▶

Arrange roses into the foam, and insert black-headed corsage pins, threaded with beads, throughout the composition.

OPPOSITE PAGE:
A glamorous orb of 'Black Magic' roses is made even more enchanting with opalescent beads that are threaded onto black-headed corsage pins and inserted into and among the velvety blooms. An elegant tussie-mussie holder and drapery tassel create a distinctive elongated profile.

FLORISTS' REVIEW

President: Frances Dudley, AAF
Publisher: Talmage McLaurin, AIFD
Floral Designer: Talmage McLaurin, AIFD
Editor: Amy Bauer
Art Director: Linda Kunkle Park
Copy Editors: Amy Bauer, David Coake
Photographers: Stephen Smith, John Collins
Creative Coordinator: James Miller, AIFD

Photos and corresponding how-to images for bouquets
on Pages 28, 30, 31, 38, 41, 42, 44, 45, 47, 56, 62, 76,
82, 86, 92, 94 and 103 by John Collins.

All other photos by Stephen Smith.

Florists' Review Wedding Bouquets was produced by
Florists' Review Enterprises, Inc.; Topeka, Kansas;
www.floristsreview.com.

Printed in China by Regent Publishing Services Ltd.
Shau Kei Wan, Hong Kong

ISBN: 978-0-9801815-3-1

Florists' Review Enterprises is the leading magazine
and book publishing company for the U.S. floral
industry. The company is home to *Florists' Review*
and *Super Floral Retailing* magazines as well as to
Florists' Review Bookstore, the industry's premier
marketplace for books and other educational materials.

For other titles from *Florists' Review*, visit our Web site,

www.floristsreview.com